Kids Wit

By Liza Charlesworth

ISBN: 978-1-339-02668-8

Art Director: Tannaz Fassihi; Designer: Tanya Chernyak
Photos ©: p6: paffy/Shutterstock.com. All other photos © Getty Images.
Copyright © Liza Charlesworth. All rights reserved. Published by Scholastic Inc.

3 4 5 6 7 8 9 10   68   32 31 30 29 28 27 26 25 24

Printed in Jiaxing, China. First printing, August 2023.

This kid has a skill.
She can skip, skip, skip!

This kid has a skill.
He can act in a skit!

It is a skill to skate
and do a big trick.

It is a skill to make a dress
with just a bit of help.

This kid can scan the sky.
She spots six ducks!

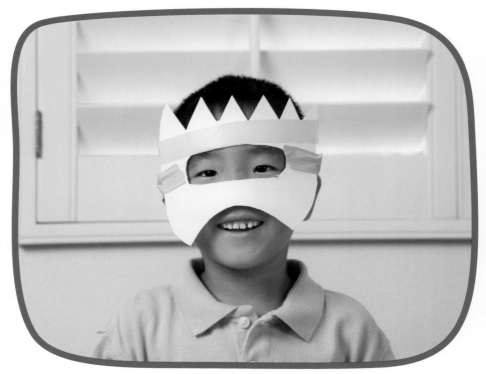

This kid can make a mask.
It is a fun, fun task.

This kid can run
and kick and score.
She has a lot of skills!